Bulldogs

by Nico Barnes

ABDO
DOGS
Kids

Visit us at www.abdopublishing.com

Published by Abdo Kids, a division of ABDO, P.O. Box 398166, Minneapolis, Minnesota 55439.

Copyright © 2015 by Abdo Consulting Group, Inc. International copyrights reserved in all countries. No part of this book may be reproduced in any form without written permission from the publisher.

Printed in the United States of America, North Mankato, Minnesota.

032014

092014

 PRINTED ON RECYCLED PAPER

Photo Credits: Shutterstock, Thinkstock

Production Contributors: Teddy Borth, Jennie Forsberg, Grace Hansen

Design Contributors: Dorothy Toth, Renée LaViolette, Laura Rask

Library of Congress Control Number: 2013952547

Cataloging-in-Publication Data

Barnes, Nico.

 Bulldogs / Nico Barnes.

  p. cm. -- (Dogs)

ISBN 978-1-62970-029-8 (lib. bdg.)

Includes bibliographical references and index.

1. Bulldogs--Juvenile literature.   I. Title.

636.72--dc23

2013952547

Table of Contents

Bulldogs

Bulldogs can look mean and grumpy. But they are **generally** kind dogs.

Bulldogs are medium-sized dogs. They are short and strong.

A bulldog's head and face are its strongest features. Its head is large and square.

A bulldog has big **wrinkles** on its face. It has a **droopy** mouth.

Bulldogs come in many colors.

Their coats are short and shiny.

Bulldog Care

Bulldogs should be brushed once a week. A bulldog's **wrinkles** should be cleaned often.

Exercise

Bulldogs should be walked daily. Be careful walking in very hot and cold weather. Bulldogs can overheat and chill easily!

17

Personality

Bulldogs are easy-going dogs.

They are happy to sit quietly

or sleep.

Bulldogs are loving and **protective**. They are great family dogs.

21

More Facts

- Warren G. Harding was the only U.S. President to have a bulldog while in office.

- Most bulldogs live about 8 to 12 years.

- Bulldogs are one of the most popular mascots for universities and sports teams.

Glossary

droopy – hanging down limply.

feature – a part of the face or body.

general – in most cases; usually.

protective – to keep safe from harm or danger.

wrinkle – a line or fold in the skin.

Index

abdokids.com

Use this code to log on to abdokids.com and access crafts, games, videos and more!

Abdo Kids Code:
DBK0298